Arne & Carlos

Easter Knits

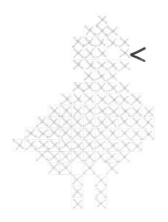

Search Press

Thanks to the women at Dale of Norway for their help knitting the patterns for the hens, rabbits, and egg cozy sweaters.

TABLE OF CONTENTS

Chapter 1
Materials...................................4

Chapter 2
The Easter Bunny...................................7

Chapter 3
Sweaters for the Easter Bunny...................................12

Chapter 4
Easter Balls and Easter Eggs...................................15

Chapter 5
Easter Ball with Skier...................................27

Chapter 6
Spring is Coming...................................35

Chapter 7
Fabergé...................................43

Chapter 8
Hens and Eggs...................................48

Chapter 9
Egg Cozy Sweaters...................................60

First published in Great Britain in 2013 by Search Press
Limited, Wellwood, North Farm Road, Tunbridge Wells, Kent
TN2 3DR

Also published in the United States of America in 2013 by
Trafalgar Square Books
North Pomfret, Vermont 05053

Originally published in Norwegian as *Påske* by Cappelen
Damm A/S

ISBN: 978-1-84448-924-4

Translation: Carol Huebscher Rhoades
Illustrations: Arne & Carlos
Photography: Ragnar Hartvig
Styling: Ingrid Skaansar
Book Design: Hanne Kjus

Printed in China

10 9 8 7 6 5 4 3 2 1

PREFACE

Well, another freezing winter has passed. We tried to dress for the cold and went outside as little as possible. Now sunshine makes a regular appearance and the water runs once again in the streams and waterfalls. We dream about spring, and summer, and long, warm days. It's time to bring out the gardening books and notes as we dream, and start planning the year's projects that, while feeling so far in the future, at the same time seem attainable at this time of year. We sow the first seeds in pots in the window box—sunflowers and squash.

By the time Easter comes, we actually dig out our winter coats again, grab our backpacks, and go up into the mountains in search of snow. The mountains call to our Scandinavian blood, and we forget, for a moment, that we scraped ice off the cars and cursed winter and the darkness for many months. These details disappear from our memories, because at Easter we want to have snow and white countryside again.

People from villages all around line up to get one last taste of winter. We warm up the mountain huts, muck out the outhouses, and freeze. Yes, even come spring, we seek out a way to freeze, so we can then make life cozy and remember that it is good to be alive. Besides, we are nearer the sun up on the mountains, and nearer the sky.

We Scandinavians are peculiar people.

Arne & Carlos

Chapter 1

MATERIALS

You'll need some basic materials in order to make the projects in this book:
Dpn (double-pointed needles), sets of 5, U.S. sizes 1.5 and 2.5, as well as 6 and 7 / 2.5 and 3 mm, as well as 4 and 4.5 mm.
• Crochet hook U.S. size C-2 or D-3 / 3 mm
• Tapestry needle for weaving in yarn
• Wool for the stuffing (carded batts)
• Yarn

These are small projects and surely you have plenty of stash yarns you can use! We used Falk, Freestyle, Heilo, Daletta, and Babyull from Dale of Norway yarn. We specify which yarn to use in the individual patterns.

Chapter 2

The Easter Bunny

You simply must have a rabbit for Easter, *this one is still wearing his winter outfit.*

7

MATERIALS

Yarn: Dale of Norway Falk (100% wool; 116 yds / 106 m, 50g) Sport weight or a similar yarn suitable for needles U.S. size 1.5 / 2.5 mm

The white rabbit is knit with Falk:

Natural white 0020

Blossom pink 4203

Nose and mouth: black 0090

Eyes: red 4018 and black 0090

1 ¾ oz / 50 g wool stuffing

BEGIN WITH THE LEFT LEG

With dpn U.S. size 1.5 / 2.5 mm, CO 8 sts and divide onto 4 dpn (2 sts per needle). Join, being careful not to twist cast-on row.

Rnd 1: K8.
Rnd 2: (K1, inc 1, k1) around.
Rnd 3: K12.
Rnd 4: (K1, inc 1, k1, inc 1, k1) around.
Rnd 5: K20.
Rnd 6: (K1, inc 1, k3, inc 1, k1) around.
Rnds 7-12: K28.
Rnd 13: (K1, k2tog, k1, k2tog, k1) around.
Rnds 14-19: K20.
Rnd 20: (K1, k2tog, k2) around.
Rnds 21-26: K16.

Begin the heel by working 6 rows stockinette (knit on RS and purl on WS) back and forth over the sts on the first needle.

Now you have a little strip on the first needle. With dpn 4, pick up and knit 4 sts along the side of the strip and place a locking ring marker (or move up beginning yarn tail) between needles 1 and 4. With dpn 2, pick up and knit 4 sts on the other side of the strip on ndl 1.

Rnd 27: Dpn 1: k4; dpn 2: k8; dpn 3: k4; dpn 4: k8.
Rnd 28: Dpn 1: k4; dpn 2: k2tog, k6; dpn 3: k4; dpn 4: k6, k2tog.

Rnd 29: Dpn 1: k4; dpn 2: k7; dpn 3: k4; dpn 4: k7.

Rnd 30: Dpn 1: k4; dpn 2: k2tog, k5; dpn 3: k4; dpn 4: k5, k2tog.

Rnd 31: Dpn 1: k4; dpn 2: k6; dpn 3: k4; dpn 4: k6.

Rnd 32: Dpn 1: k4; dpn 2: k2tog, k4; dpn 3: k4; dpn 4: k4, k2tog.

Rnd 33: Dpn 1: k4; dpn 2: k5; dpn 3: k4; dpn 4: k5.

Rnd 34: Dpn 1: k4; dpn 2: k2tog, k3: dpn 3: k4; dpn 4: k3, k2tog.

Rnd 35: K16.

Rnd 36: (K1, k2tog, k1) around.

Stuff the foot with wool.

Rnds 37-67: K12 (= 30 rounds).

Rnd 68: K1, inc 1, k10, inc 1, k1.

Rnd 69: K14.

Rnd 70: K1, inc 1, k12, inc 1, k1.

Rnd 71: K16.

Rnd 72: BO 2, k12 (including last st from bind-off), BO 2.

Divide leg sts onto 2 dpn (6 sts per needle).

RIGHT LEG

Work as for Rnds 1-67 of left leg.

Rnd 68: K5, inc 1, k2, inc 1, k5.

Rnd 69: K14.

Rnd 70: K6, inc 1, k2, inc 1, k6.

Rnd 71: K16.

Rnd 72: K6, BO 4, k6 (including last st from bind-off).

Divide leg sts onto 2 dpn (6 sts per needle). Stuff legs with wool.

JOIN THE LEGS AND KNIT THE BODY

Rnd 1: Continue knitting with the strand of yarn from the right leg: Dpn 1: k6 from right leg; dpn 2 and 3: k6 from left leg; dpn 4: k6 from right leg.

Move the marker up to the side here.

Now the bound-off 4 sts on each leg should face each other between the legs.

Rnds 2-23: K24 (= 22 rounds).

Rnd 24: BO 2 sts, k8 (including the last st of bind-off), BO 4, k8 (including last st of bind-off), BO 2.

Place sts of front and back onto separate needles.

KNIT THE ARMS

With dpn U.S. 1.5 / 2.5 mm, CO 6 sts and divide sts onto 3 dpn. Join, being careful not to twist cast-on row.

Rnd 1: K6.

Rnd 2: (K1, inc 1, k1) around.

Rnd 3: K9.

Rnd 4: (K1, inc 1, k1, inc 1, k1) around.

Rnd 5: K15.

Rnd 6: (K1, inc 1, k3, inc 1, k1) around.

Rnds 7-13: K21.

Rnd 14: (K1, k2tog, k1, k2tog, k1) around.

Rnd 15: K15.

Rnd 16: (K1, k2tog, k2) around.

Rnd 17: K12.

Rnd 18: (K1, k2tog, k1) around.

Rnds 19-40: K9 (= 22 rnds).

Rnd 41: BO 2, k5 (including last st after bind-off), BO 2.

Put the arm sts on a holder and make the other arm the same way.

KNIT THE BODY AND ARMS TOGETHER ON 4 DPN

Rnd 1: Back: K8; left arm: k5; front: k8; right arm: k5.

Rnd 2: Back: K1, k2tog, k2, k2tog, k1; arm: k5; front: k1, k2tog, k2, k2tog, k1; arm: k5.

Rnd 3: K22.

Rnd 4: Back: K2, k2tog, k2; arm: k5; front: k2, k2tog, k2; arm: k5.

Rnd 5: K20.

Rnd 6: (K1, k2tog, k2) around.

Rnd 7: K16.

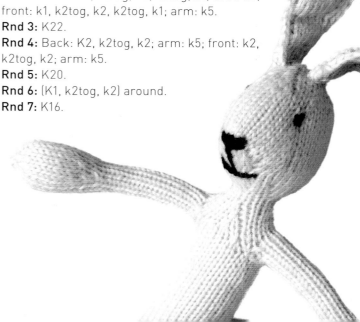

Rnd 8: (K1, k2tog, k1) around = 12 sts remain.

Seam the underarms and stuff the arms and body with wool.
Rnds 9-12: Knit.

BEGIN HEAD
Rnd 13: (K1, inc 1, k1, inc 1, k1) around.
Rnd 14: K20.
Rnd 15: (K1, inc 1, k3, inc 1, k1) around.
Rnd 16: K28.
Rnd 17: (K1, inc 1, k5, inc 1, k1) around.
Rnd 18: K36.
Rnd 19: Dpn 1: K9; dpn 2: k11 onto the needle; dpn 3: k5; dpn 4: place the 2 last sts on needle 3 onto ndl 4 and k11.
Rnd 20: K20; dpn 3 shade head with short rows: k5; turn and p5; turn, k5; turn and p5; turn, k5; turn and p5; turn, k5; turn and p5. Now, with dpn 2, pick up and knit 5 sts on the side of the strip on dpn 3. On the other side of the strip with dpn 4, pick up and knit 5 sts. K21 to finish round.
Rnd 21: K46.
Rnd 22: K17, k2tog, k17, k2tog, k8.
Rnd 23: K44.
Rnd 24: K17, k2tog, k15, k2tog, k8.
Rnd 25: K42.
Rnd 26: K17, k2tog, k13, k2tog, k8.
Rnd 27: K40.
Move 2 sts from dpn 2 onto dpn 3 and move 2 sts from dpn 4 to dpn 3.
Rnd 28: K17, k2tog, k11, k2tog, k8.
Rnd 29: K38.
Rnd 30: K17, k2tog, k9, k2tog, k8.
Rnd 31: K36.
Rnd 32: (K1, k2tog, k3, k2tog, k1) around.
Rnd 33: K28.
Rnd 34: (K1, k2tog, k1, k2tog, k1) around.
Rnd 35: K20.
Rnd 36: (K1, k2tog, k2) around.
Rnd 37: K16.
Rnd 38: (K1, k2tog, k1) around.

Cut yarn and pull end through remaining 12 sts. Fill with wool.
Pull tail through remaining sts once more and weave in ends to WS.

EMBROIDERING ON THE MOUTH AND NOSE
Sew 4 stitches for the tip of the nose, then make a straight line of back stitches down to the mouth (where you can see the shift in the knitting from the strip that was knit back and forth); at that line, embroider the mouth with back stitches.

EARS FOR THE RABBIT
Each ear is made with 2 layers, one knit with Blossom pink 4203 and the other in the same color as for the rabbit body, for example Natural white 0020. The ears are worked in stockinette: knit on the RS and purl on the WS. With needles U.S. 1.5 / 2.5 mm, CO 5 sts.
Row 1 (WS): P5.
Row 2: K5.
Row 3: P5.
Row 4: K5.
Row 5: P5.
Row 6: K1, inc 1, k3, inc 1, k1.
Rows 7-13: Continue in stockinette with knit on RS and purl on WS.
Row 14: K1, inc 1, k5, inc 1, k1.
Rows 15-27: Continue in stockinette with knit on RS and purl on WS.
Row 28: K1, k2tog, k3, k2tog, k1.
Row 29: P7.
Row 30: K1, k2tog, k1, k2tog, k1.
Row 31: P5.
Row 32: K1, k2tog, k2.
Row 33: P4.
Row 34: K1, k2tog, k1.
Row 35: P3.
Row 36: BO knitwise.

Gently seam press the two parts of the ear and lay them together with WS facing WS. Crochet the two pieces together with single crochet into the outermost stitches around. Crochet with the skin color side facing you.
Make the other ear the same way.
Sew the ears to the head, approx. 3/8 in / 1 cm from each other on each side of the finishing at the top of the head.

EYES

Embroider the eyes with your choice of color and cross stitch where the decreases were made over the nose.

With black, embroider a small seed stitch at the center of the cross stitch.

Make a pom-pon tail to sew on the back.

With such a lovely pom-pon tail on his backside, the rabbit doesn't need to wear any pants.

Make a pom-pon to sew onto the back.

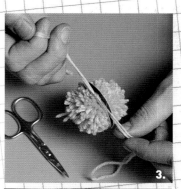

1. Draw two circles on paper. We traced ours with an egg cup. Cut a small hole in the center.

2. Hold the two pieces of paper together and wrap yarn around them, using a tapestry needle. Cut the yarn by inserting the scissors' tip between the paper circles.

3. Tie a strong double strand of thread securely between the two circles.

4. Remove the paper circles and trim the pom-pon before sewing it on.

Chapter 3

Sweaters
for the Easter Bunny

We decided to make just one garment for the Easter Bunny, a sweater knitted with a heavy yarn. The sizes of the stitches on the sweater are in proportion to the rabbit's size. The sweater was knit so that it must be pulled on with the legs up in the sweater first and then pulled on. With the pom-pon tail, it was easier without pants but if you want, you can knit the legs and half of the body with another color than the skin color and the use the skin color for the pom-pon tail to give an illusion of pants.

Everyone knows a couple of rabbits multiply quickly and before you know it, you will have an armful.

MATERIALS

Yarn: Dale of Norway Freestyle (100% wool; 87 yds / 80 m, 50g) Worsted

Set of 5 dpn U.S. sizes 7 and 8 / 4.5 and 5 mm

BODY

With smaller needles, CO 24 sts and divide evenly over 4 dpn = 6 sts per dpn. Join, being careful not to twist cast-on row.

Work 4 rnds k2, p2 rib.

Change to larger dpn.

Rnds 1-3: Knit.

Rnd 4: BO 2 sts, k8 (including last st from bind-off), BO 4, k8 (including last st from bind-off), BO 2. Place 8 sts for front on one needle and 8 sts for back on another needle.

SLEEVES

With smaller dpn, CO 12 sts and divide onto 3 dpn (= 4 sts per needle); join.

Work 4 rnds k2, p2 rib.

Change to larger needles.

Rnds 1-7: Knit.

Rnd 8: BO 2, k8 (including last st from bind-off), BO 2.

Place sleeve sts on a holder and then make another sleeve the same way.

Divide the body and sleeve sts onto larger dpn: 8 sts for back on one needle, 8 sts left sleeve on ndl 2, 8 sts front on ndl 3, 8 sts right sleeve on ndl 4.

Rnd 1: K32.

Rnd 2: (K1, k2tog, k2, k2tog, k1) around.

Rnd 3: K24.

Rnd 4: Change to smaller needles and work (k2, p2) around.

Work 3 more rnds k2, p2 rib.

BO and cut yarn. Seam underarms. Weave in ends neatly on WS. Gently steam press sweater except for ribbing.

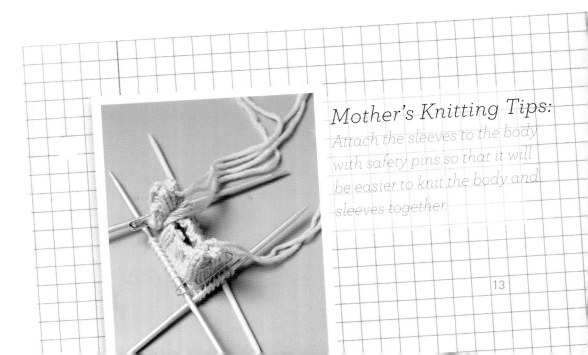

Mother's Knitting Tips:
Attach the sleeves to the body with safety pins so that it will be easier to knit the body and sleeves together.

13

Chapter 4

Easter Balls
and Easter Eggs

In 2010, we published our book, *55 Christmas Balls to Knit*, which became a huge success. And then everyone wanted more balls to knit, in 2011, many people knitted the so-called "baby balls"—pink and light blue balls to hang up under the hood of a baby carriage. So, right before Easter we decided to design Easter balls and Easter eggs. This ball with the chick was made especially for an Easter report in the Oppland Worker's paper last year.

MATERIALS
Yarn: Dale of Norway
Heilo (100% wool;
108 yds / 100 m, 50 g)
DK / Sport
Petrol blue 7062
Sunglow yellow 2126
Mist blue 5813
Red 4018

15

You'll find several balls in "*55 Christmas Balls to Knit*" that would also make wonderful Easter decorations, just choose colors suitable for Easter. The motifs were inspired by plants, birds, skiers, and all sorts of snow crystals, ornaments, and motifs from old knitted garments. There's room for creativity here. The basic pattern for Easter eggs and Easter balls is at the back of this book on pages 62 & 63.

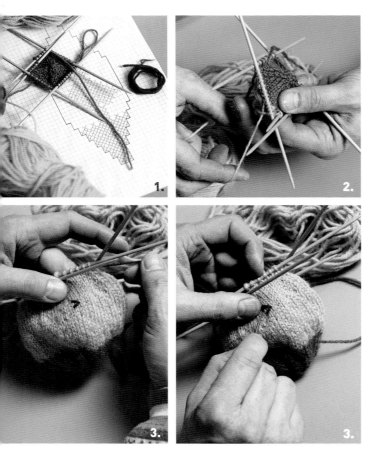

1. Easter balls and Easter eggs are made with the same basic guidelines. The charts are repeated over 4 needles. Sew up the hole at the beginning and use the tail as a marking thread.

2. When there are long stretches between the pattern stitches, as on the chicken's legs, twist the pattern yarns on the back (wrong side) while you knit with the main color. This helps prevent the yarns from drawing in too much and the knitting will be more even.

3. When a color is only used for very small areas, it is easier to embroider that color on with duplicate stitch and you'll avoid tangled yarns and long floats.

4. The balls and eggs are filled with carded wool after being knitted and steamed. The wool makes the balls and eggs easy to shape well, springy and light.

5. After the hole at the top has been sewn together, crochet a loop with 30 chain sts for the hanging loop. The ends are then threaded through the ball or egg and sewn securely to the base.

MATERIALS

Yarn: Dale of Norway
Falk (100% wool; 116 yds /
106 m, 50 g) Sport
Cocoa brown 3072
Sand 2611
Burnt orange 3418

Rabbits *and* Eggs

In some places it is traditional for children to hunt for Easter eggs. It is rather remarkable that the Easter Rabbit is the one who hides the eggs around the house and yard. The connection between the Easter Rabbit and Easter eggs must have something to do with fertility. Eggs, like rabbits and hares, are viewed as fertility symbols of new life during the Spring season.

This rabbit has a bucket full of eggs and is ready to hide them.

Hares
around an Egg

MATERIALS

Yarn: Dale of Norway Heilo
(100% wool; 108 yds / 100 m,
50 g) DK / Sport

Petrol blue 7062

Natural white 0020

Dark salmon 4624

Sunglow yellow 2126

Pure white 0010

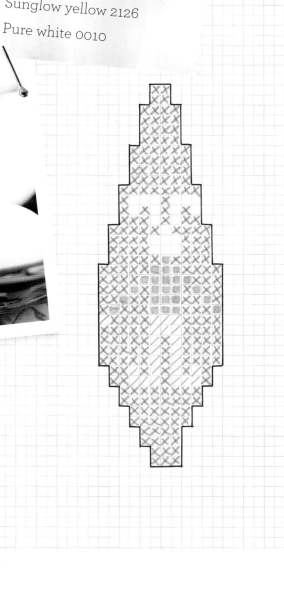

Just as Grandfather Rabbit from Rabbittown showed the children where they could get inspiration for their eggs, we wanted to show what we took our inspiration from. We found the idea for this first egg in a story about Grandfather Rabbit.

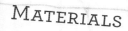

MATERIALS

Yarn: Dale of Norway Heilo (100% wool; 108 yds / 100 m, 50 g) DK / Sport

Mist blue 5813

Natural white 0020

Red 4018

Sunglow yellow 2126

Black 0090

Use designs painted
by children to knit on
the eggs.

Egg
*with dots, simple
and pretty.*

MATERIALS

Yarn: Dale of Norway Heilo
(100% wool; 108 yds / 100 m,
50 g) DK / Sport
Light sheep heather 2931
Pumpkin 3237
Red 4018
Sunglow yellow 2126
Asparagus green 9145
Norwegian blue 5744

MATERIALS

Yarn: Dale of Norway Babyull
(100% Merino wool; 180 yds /
165 m, 50 g) Fingering
Lagoon blue 6435
Pastel yellow 2303
Tangerine orange 2817
Red 3718

Little crosses in five different colors against a single-colored background for a very simple and decorative egg.

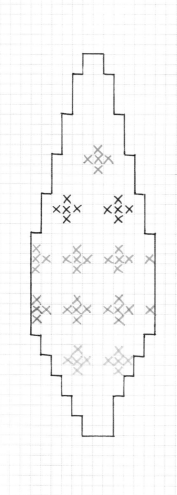

MATERIALS

Yarn: Dale of Norway Heilo
(100% wool; 108 yds / 100 m,
50 g) DK / Sport

Norwegian blue 5744

Sunglow yellow 2126

Blossom pink 4203

Mist blue 5813

Plum smoke 5062

MATERIALS

Yarn: Dale of Norway Heilo
(100% wool; 108 yds / 100 m,
50 g) DK / Sport

Mist blue 5813

Blossom pink 4203

Red 4018

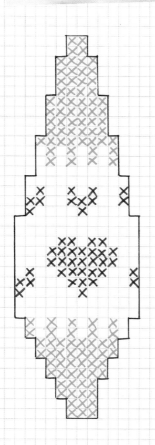

The heart is one of children's
favorite motifs, and, with red
and pink, it couldn't be better.

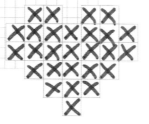

I tie up my sack,

I fasten on my skis,

As soon as the light brightens the sky.

Away from the chimney corner!

So happy and so free.

Towards the large white forest,

I'm on my way.

Margrethe Munthe

Chapter 5

Easter Ball
with Skier

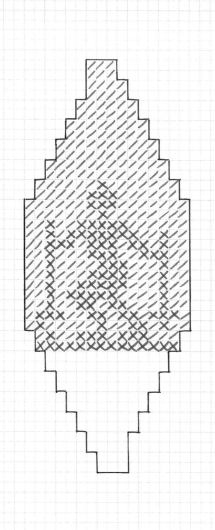

MATERIALS

Yarn: Dale of Norway
Heilo (100% wool; 108 yds
/ 100 m, 50 g) DK / Sport

Pure white 0010

Red 4018

Mist blue 5813

A Little RABBIT on Cross Country Skis

A small and very tired rabbit sees a hut in the distance, only a bit more to go on his cross country skis. Someone else has gotten there before

him, so lucky for him the hut will be warm
and cozy. Now it's time to relax by a warm
crackling fire and enjoy hot cocoa and
something good to eat.

Going out on a ski run in the twilight
is both pleasant and sometimes a little
exhausting but an evening with good
friends at the hut makes it all worthwhile.

Egg
with Outhouse

You can sit here with your
own thoughts, at least until
someone knocks on the door.

MATERIALS

Yarn: Dale of Norway Heilo
(100% wool; 108 yds / 100 m,
50 g) DK / Sport
Pure white 0010
Mist blue 5813
Norwegian blue 5744
Red 4018

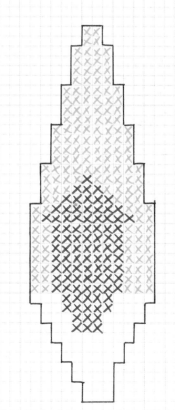

*This rabbit has put away the Christmas
decorations and set out the Easter
ones. The wood is chopped and the
outhouse has been mucked out.*

Evening Red
gives sweet days

MATERIALS

Yarn: Dale of Norway Heilo
(100% wool; 108 yds / 100 m,
50 g) DK / Sport
Norwegian blue 5744
Red 4018
Pumpkin 3237
Sunglow yellow 2126
Mist blue 5813

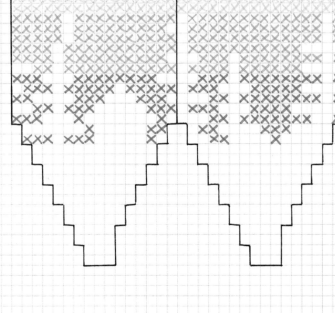

Morning Red
gives wet days

MATERIALS

Yarn: Dale of Norway Heilo (100% wool; 108 yds / 100 m, 50 g) DK / Sport

Pure white 0010

Red 4018

Pumpkin 3237

Sunglow yellow 2126

Mist blue 5813

Chapter 6

Spring
is Coming

With Easter, spring arrives and the snow is melting away. The rivers and streams overflow their banks and the sun rises far above the horizon. The smell of the fertile earth and the longer days make life easier and full of expectations. The first spring flowers push through the snow and greet the sunshine. The rabbit has plenty to do: and a nice long Easter break to tidy up the yard.

Spring Onions
in a blue pot

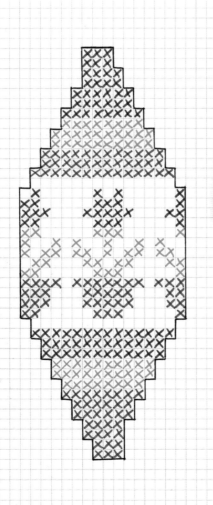

MATERIALS

Yarn: Dale of Norway Heilo
(100% wool; 108 yds / 100 m,
50 g) DK / Sport
Soft blue 5943
Asparagus green 9145
Dark salmon 4624
Natural white 0020

Ball
with flowers

MATERIALS

Yarn: Dale of Norway
Heilo (100% wool; 108 yds
/ 100 m, 50 g) DK / Sport
Light sheep heather 2931
Asparagus green 9145

MATERIALS

Yarn: Dale of Norway Heilo (100%
wool; 108 yds / 100 m, 50 g) DK / Sport
Pure white 0010
Asparagus green 9145
Sunglow yellow 2126

Ball
*with a red tulip in
a cracked egg*

MATERIALS

Yarn: Dale of Norway Heilo
(100% wool; 108 yds / 100 m,
50 g) DK / Sport

Mist blue 5813

Asparagus green 9145

Red 4018

Pure white 0010

Plum smoke 5062

Egg
with a simple flower motif that can be varied endlessly

MATERIALS

Yarn: Dale of Norway Heilo
(100% wool; 108 yds / 100 m,
50 g) DK / Sport
Mist blue 5813
Pumpkin 3237
Red 4018

MATERIALS

Yarn: Dale of Norway Babyull
(100% Merino wool; 180 yds /
165 m, 50 g) Fingering
Pastel yellow 2203
Lagoon blue 6435
Tangerine orange 2817

39

Egg
with little tulips

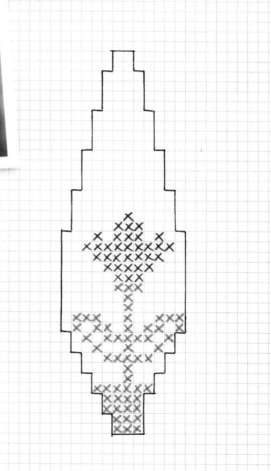

MATERIALS

Yarn: Dale of Norway Heilo
(100% wool; 108 yds / 100 m,
50 g) DK / Sport

Pure white 0010

Asparagus green 9145

Plum smoke 5062

Sunglow yellow flower 2126

Red flower 4018

*We've knitted several tulip
variations here.*

Chapter 7

Fabergé

Peter Carl Fabergé was a 19th-century Russian jeweler who made spectacular objects in enamel and gemstones. For a long time, he sold enameled eggs set with diamonds, rubies, and sapphires to the Russian royal house which the Czar presented to the Czarinna. We have a collection of Fabergé eggs but ours are metal with pressed patterns representing diamonds and other expensive materials. We've been inspired by our metal eggs and knitted our own versions of Fabergé eggs.

MATERIALS

Yarn: Dale of Norway Heilo
(100% wool; 108 yds / 100 m,
50 g) DK / Sport

Mist gray 2425

Wine 4246

Green 7076

Eggs

with ornamentation inspired by Fabergé eggs

This egg is decorated
with three colors.
The blue stitches are
embroidered on with
duplicate stitch.

MATERIALS

Yarn: Dale of Norway Heilo
(100% wool; 108 yds / 100
m, 50 g) DK / Sport
Pumpkin 3237
Wine 4246
Soft blue 5943

Ball with a motif inspired by a knitted swimsuit from *Every Woman's Knitting Book*, published in 1947. You might think that there is a mistake in the pattern on Row 11, but we have drawn in one less cross on the right side to allow for a smooth transition after the increases on Row 12. So, don't knit an extra pattern stitch, and the design will look the same on both sides. We have tried the pattern with the extra stitch and it simply doesn't align smoothly following the increase.

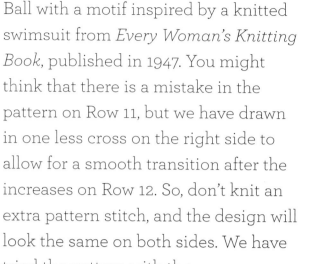

MATERIALS

Yarn: Dale of Norway Heilo (100% wool; 108 yds / 100 m, 50 g) DK / Sport

Mist gray 2425

Norwegian blue 5744

MATERIALS

Yarn: Dale of Norway Heilo (100% wool; 108 yds / 100 m, 50 g) DK / Sport

Dark salmon 4624

Norwegian blue 5744

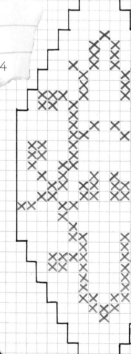

45

This pattern could just as well be from an old ski sweater as from the decoration on an old Fabergé egg. There are many colors to manage but it comes out really nice.

MATERIALS

Yarn: Dale of Norway Heilo (100% wool; 108 yds / 100 m, 50 g) DK / Sport

Mist blue 5813

Norwegian blue 5744

Red 4018

Sunglow yellow 2126

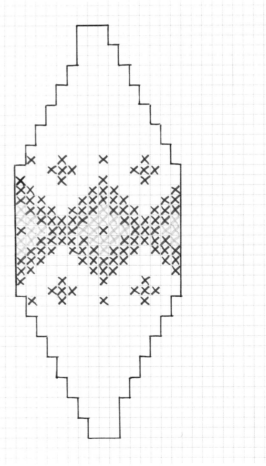

This ball with large circles is knitted with three colors and opens the possibilities for many variations.

MATERIALS

Yarn: Dale of Norway Heilo (100% wool; 108 yds / 100 m, 50 g) DK / Sport

Red 4018

Blossom pink 4203

Navy blue 5563

MATERIALS

Yarn: Dale of Norway Heilo (100% wool; 108 yds / 100 m, 50 g) DK / Sport

Petrol blue 7062

Pumpkin 3237

Sunglow yellow 2126

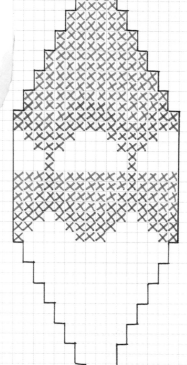

Hens and eggs

Small eggs, the same size as regular eggs, knitted
with Babyull and needles U.S. size 1.5 / 2.5 mm.

Egg
with a pink hen

MATERIALS

Yarn: Dale of Norway Heilo
(100% wool; 108 yds / 100 m,
50 g) DK / Sport
Red 4018
Blossom pink 4203

The only chicken in the basket,
An old hen from an embroidery,
fits perfectly on the egg.

MATERIALS

Yarn: Dale of Norway Babyull
(100% Merino wool; 180 yds /
165 m, 50 g) Fingering
Pastel yellow 2203
Tangerine orange 2817

Chick in the Egg Shell

*Red and blue stitches
are embroidered on*

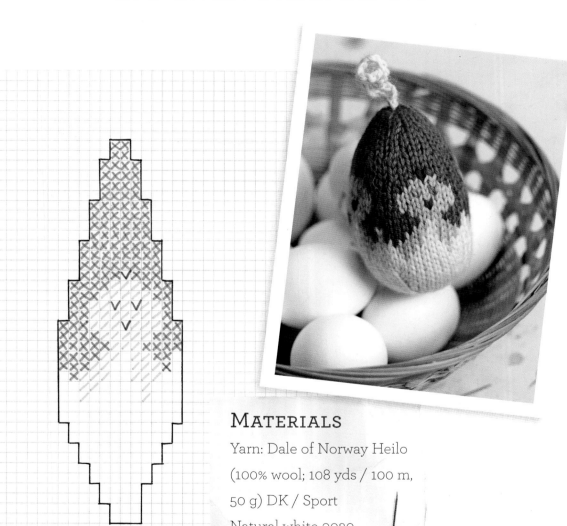

MATERIALS

Yarn: Dale of Norway Heilo
(100% wool; 108 yds / 100 m,
50 g) DK / Sport
Natural white 0020
Sunglow yellow 2126
Asparagus green 9145
Soft blue 5943
Red 4018

Blue Hens

We found these hens on a
vintage children's mitten.

MATERIALS

Yarn: Dale of Norway Heilo
(100% wool; 108 yds / 100 m,
50 g) DK / Sport
Sunglow yellow 2126
Red 4018
Pure white 0010
Norwegian blue 5744

Hens

A hen with crocheted feathers on her wings and around her stomach. This chicken can be knitted in many colors, ours is brown and yellow, like a Brahma chicken named Gunhild that we had before she changed her home and her name. Now she is called Gullkula.

MATERIALS

Yarn: Dale of Norway Falk (100% wool; 116 yds / 106 m, 50 g) DK / Sport

Cocoa brown 3072

Dandelion yellow 2417

Goldenrod 2427

Red 4018

Two sets of 5 dpn U.S. size 1.5 / 2.5 mm

Crochet hook US size C-2 or D-3 / 3 mm

With three dpn and goldenrod 2427, make the claws as follows:

CO 4 sts divided onto 2 needles. Hold the needles parallel and join to work in the round. Knit 10 rnds. Leave the finished claw on the 2 needles and make another one with 2 more dpn.
When the second claw is finished, put the stitches onto the needle with the first claw. Knit the third claw the same way and then put the stitches onto the same needle holding the first and second ones.

JOIN THE CLAWS WITH 4 DPN
Knit the first 3 sts on the needle nearest you with dpn 1.
Knit the last 3 sts from the needle nearest you onto dpn 2.
Knit the next 3 sts on the second needle onto dpn 3.
Knit the last 3 sts onto dpn 4.

Knit 4 rounds:
Closing any holes, weave in all the ends between and in the tips of the claws.

Rnd 5: Place the first 6 sts onto 1 dpn and then, working back and forth, work 4 rows in stockinette (a small heel flap) over these 6 sts.

SMALL CLAW ON BACK OF FOOT
CO 4 sts on 2 new dpn; join and knit 6 rounds for a small claw.

Move the 4 sts onto one needle:
The 1st st from the back needle, the 2nd st from the front needle, the 3rd st from the back needle, and the 4th st from the front needle. K2tog twice. Cut yarn and weave in end from claw.
Place the 6 sts from the heel onto one dpn together with the sts from the little claw in this order: 2 sts from the heel, 1 st from the little claw, 1 st from the heel, 1 st from the little claw, 3 sts from the heel.

The eternal question: which came first? There is no doubt here. The chick has broken free and will soon be completely out of the egg.

CONTINUE KNITTING THE FOOT
With another dpn, pick up and knit 3 sts along the side of the heel; with a third dpn, pick up and knit 3 sts on the other side of the heel.
You should now have 2 dpn with 6 sts each and a little claw with 8 sts.
Continue, working the foot sts divided over 3 dpn.
Rnd 1: Dpn 1: K2, k2tog, k2tog, k2; dpn 2 and 3: k6 on each needle.
Rnd 2: K18.
Rnd 3: (K1, k2tog, k2tog, k1) on each needle.
Rnd 4: K12.
Rnd 5: (K1, k2tog, k1) on each needle.
Rnds 6-40: Knit. Fill the leg with wool as you work.
Rnd 41: K2, BO 2, K5 (including last stitch from bind-off).

A first look at the world outside.

Rnd 1: K14.
Rnd 2: K14.
Rnd 3: (K1, inc 1) around.
Rnd 4: K28.
Rnd 5: Knit and rearrange the sts so there are 7 sts on each dpn.
Rnd 6: (K1, inc 1, k5, inc 1, k1) around.
Rnd 7: K36.
Rnd 8: (K1, inc 1, k7, inc 1, k1) around.
Rnd 9: K44.

Seam the groin and fill with wool.

Rnd 10: (K1, inc 1, k9, inc 1, k1) around.
Rnd 11: K52.
Rnd 12: (K1, inc 1, k11, inc 1, k1) around.
Rnds 13-23: K60.
Rnd 24: (K1, k2tog, k9, k2tog, k1) around.
Rnd 25: K52.
Rnd 26: K52.
Rnd 27: (K1, k2tog, k7, k2tog, k1) around.
Rnd 28: K44.
Rnd 29: K44.
Rnd 30: (K1, k2tog, k5, k2tog, k1) around.
Rnd 31: K36.
Rnd 32: K36.
Rnd 33: (K1, k2tog, k3, k2tog, k1) around.
Rnds 34-37: K28.
Rnd 38: (K1, k2tog, k1, k2tog, k1) around.
Rnds 39-44: K20.
Rnd 45: K3, BO 4, k6 (including last st from bind-off), BO 4, k3 (including last st from bind-off).

KNIT THE HEN'S WINGS
With dpn U.S. size 1.5 / 2.5 mm, CO 20 sts; divide onto 4 dpn and join.
Rnds 1-2: K20.
Rnd 3: (K1, inc 1, k8, inc 1, k1) around.
Rnds 4-5: K24.
Rnd 6: (K1, inc 1, k10, inc 1, k1) around.
Rnds 7-8: K28.
Rnd 9: (K1, inc 1, k12, inc 1, k1) around.
Rnds 10-11: K32.
Rnd 12: (K1, inc 1, k14, inc 1, k1) around.
Rnds 13-18: K36.
Rnd 19: (K1, k2tog, k12, k2tog, k1) around.

Knit the second foot as for the first through Rnd 41.
After the little claw is joined to the foot, begin with 3 sts from the foot: Place the 6 heel sts on a needle together with the sts from the little claw in this order: 2 sts from heel, 1 st from little claw, 1 st from heel, 1 st from little claw, 2 sts from heel.

Rnd 41: BO 2 sts and k7 (including last st from bind-off).

Divide the leg sts over 4 dpn, with 2 dpn for each leg, 3 sts on the back needles and 4 sts on the front needles. Join the legs and, at the same time, change to cocoa brown or whatever color you'd like your hen to be. Begin at the center back (the small claw faces you).

Rnds 20-22: K32.
Rnd 23: (K1, k2tog, k10, k2tog, k1) around.
Rnds 24-26: K28.
Rnd 27: (K1, k2tog, k8, k2tog, k1) around.
Rnds 28-30: K24.
Rnd 31: (K1, k2tog, k6, k2tog, k1) around.
Rnds 32-34: K20.
Rnd 35: (K1, k2tog, k4, k2tog, k1) around.
Rnds 36-38: K16.
Rnd 39: (K1, k2tog, k2, k2tog, k1) around.
Rnds 40-42: K12.
Rnd 43: K1, k2tog, k2tog, k1, k6.
Rnds 44-46: K10.
Rnd 47: BO 4, k6.
Move all the wing sts to one needle and make the other wing the same way.

Join the wings and body.
Rnd 1: Begin at the back and k6, right wing k6, front k6, left wing k6.
Rnd 2: (K1, k2tog, k2tog, k1) on each needle around.
Rnd 3: K16.
Seam below the wings.
Rnd 4: (K1, k2tog, k1) on each needle around.
Knit 2 rounds for the neck.

HEAD
Rnd 1: (K1, inc 1, k1, inc 1, k1) around.
Rnd 2: K20.
Rnd 3: (K1, inc 1, k3, inc 1, k1) around.
Rnd 4: K28.
Rnd 5: (K1, inc 1, k5, inc 1, k1) around.
Rnds 6-9: K36.
Fill the body and head with wool.
Rnd 10: (K1, k2tog, k3, k2tog, k1) around.
Rnd 11: K28.
Rnd 12: (K1, k2tog, k1, k2tog, k1) around.
Rnd 13: K20.
Rnd 14: (K1, k2tog, k2) around.
Rnd 15: K16.
Rnd 16: (K1, k2tog, k1) around.
Cut yarn and pull end through remaining 12 sts; fill head with wool.
Bring yarn through live sts again and pull tight to close hole at top.

The hen has embroidered eyes and a crocheted beak and comb.

Use yellow to crochet the beak at the center front: Ch 3, 3 tr, end by joining the three sts with a single crochet through all 3 sts. Cut yarn and weave in ends.

CROCHETED RED COMB
At the center of the head, with red, work 4 ch loops: (1 sc into head, ch 3) 4 times and end with 1 sc in the head. Turn and work 4 dc in each loop. Cut yarn and weave in ends.

EYES
Sew three long stitches in a fan out from the point where you'd like to place each eye. With desired color, make a little cross stitch at the base of the "fan." Use black to make a small "dot" with a seed stitch at the center of the cross stitch.

The wings are decorated with chain stitch loops and double crochet into the loops.

Crochet 10 lines of chain loops on the wings, from the lower edge to the top where the decreases on the wing end. Space the lines approx 3/8 in / 1 cm apart. Work each loop with (1 sc in the wing, ch 5), repeat and end with 1 sc in the wing. Turn and work ch 3 (= 1 tr) and then 4 tr in each loop.

1st row: At the bottom edge of the wing tip, work 2 loops.
2nd row: 3 loops.
3rd row: 4 loops.
4th row: 6 loops.
5th row: 5 loops.
6th row: 4 loops.
7th row: 3 loops.
8th row: 2 loops.
9th row: 2 loops.
10th row: 1 loop.
Our hen also has crocheted loops around her stomach for a little flared skirt.

Crochet 4 rows of chain loops around the stomach of the hen, beginning where the color changes from the legs to the stomach.
1st row: 8 loops.
2nd row: 12 loops.
3rd row: 17 loops.
4th row: 18 loops.

Work 4 tr between each dc of the 3 center dc groups at center back, on the 3rd and 4th rows.
Begin row with ch 4 and 3 tr in first loop, and then work 4 tr in each loop across.

It's a struggle getting out of the egg so a little nap afterwards in the nesting box is in order.

Chapter 9

Egg Cozy Sweaters

Keep your egg warm
with a hand knit
sweater. Knit one in
you college colors
or add stripes.

Use duplicate stitch to
embroider the initial of the
person getting the egg. Our
egg cozy sweaters each have
our initials A and C. Yellow
2015 sweater has a red 4018
letter while the pink 4516
sweater has blue 5473 letter.

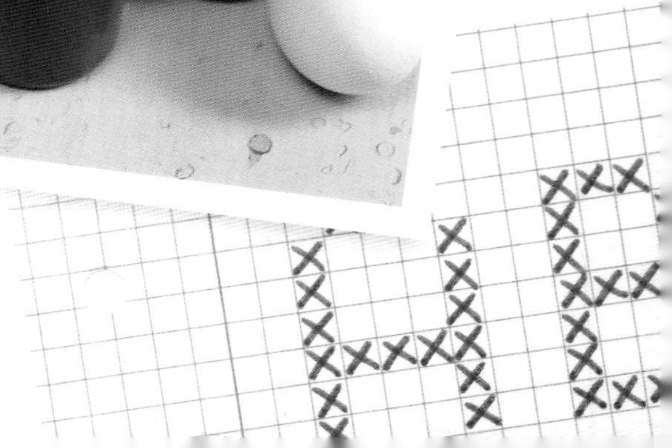

MATERIALS

Yarn: Dale of Norway Dalette (100% wool; 153 yds / 141 m, 50 g) Fingering

Sets of 5 dpn U.S. sizes 1.5 and 2.5 / 2.5 and 3 mm

This striped sweater changes color every 2 rounds.

BODY

With dpn U.S. size 1.5 / 2.5 mm, CO 40 sts and divide evenly over 4 dpn = 10 sts per needle. Join, being careful not to twist cast-on row. Work 6 rounds k1, p1 rib. Change to larger needles and continue:

Rnd 1: K40.
Rnd 2: (K1, sl 1, k1, psso, k14, k2tog, k1) around.
Rnd 3: K36.
Rnd 4: (K1, sl 1, k1, psso, k12, k2tog, k1) around.
Rnd 5: K32.
Rnd 6: (K1, sl 1, k1, psso, k10, k2tog, k1) around.
Rnd 7: K28.
Rnd 8: (K1, sl 1, k1, psso, k8, k2tog, k1) around.
Rnd 9: K24.
Rnd 10: BO 2, k8 (including last st from bind-off), BO 4, k8 (including last st from bind-off), BO 2.

Place sts of back and front each on separate needles.

SLEEVES

With smaller needles, CO 12 sts and divide evenly over 4 dpn = 3 sts per needle. Join and work in k1, p1 rib for 6 rnds.
Change to larger needles and knit 9 rounds.
Rnd 10: BO 2, k8 (including last st from bind-off), BO 2.
Place sleeve sts onto a dpn and put aside.
Make the other sleeve the same way.

Join the body and sleeves.

Rnd 1: K32.
Rnd 2: *K1, k2tog, k2, k2tog, k1*; rep * to * around.
Rnd 3: K24.
Rnd 4: *K1, k2tog, k2tog, k1*; rep * to * around.
Rnd 5: K16.

Change to smaller needles and work neck in k2, p2 rib for 15 rounds.
Bind off in rib. Weave in all ends neatly on WS and seam underarms.

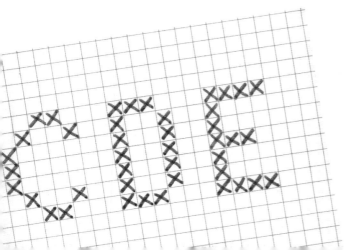

Easter Balls

BASIC PATTERN

This pattern is the basis for all the balls. The charted motif for each individual ball is designed to work within this basic pattern. Don't forget that the charts only show the stitches for ¼ of the ball. The chart stitches are repeated on each of the 4 double-pointed needles. The first row of 3 stitches on the chart represents the 3 cast-on stitches and is not knitted again. The top 3 stitches are not worked either. On the last round, cut the yarn and pull the tail through the remaining 12 stitches, pull tight and weave in tail on WS. Most of the patterns are divided over 4 dpn but some of the balls have patterns only over 2 needles. In that case, the chart shows two repeats side-by-side.

Work as follows:
Rnd 1 (the bottom row on the chart with 3 blocks): Cast on 12 sts over dpn US 2.5 / 3 mm. Divide these 12 sts over 4 dpn = 3 sts per ndl.
Rnd 2: Knit 12.
Rnd 3: (K2, inc 1, k1) on each ndl. [Note: see page 65 for how to increase]
Rnd 4: Knit 16.
Rnd 5: (K1, inc 1, k2, inc 1, k1) on each ndl.
Rnd 6: Knit 24.
Rnd 7: (K1, inc 1, k4, inc 1, k1) on each ndl.
Rnd 8: Knit 32.
Rnd 9: (K1, inc 1, k6, inc 1, k1) on each ndl.
Rnd 10: Knit 40.
Rnd 11: (K1, inc 1, k8, inc 1, k1) on each ndl.
Rnd 12: Knit 48.
Rnd 13: (K1, inc 1, k10, inc 1, k1) on each ndl.
Rnd 14: Knit 56.
Rnd 15: (K1, inc 1, k12, inc 1, k1) on each ndl.
Rnds 16-27: Knit 64.
Rnd 28: (K1, k2tog, k10, k2tog, k1) on each ndl.
Rnd 29: Knit 56.
Rnd 30: (K1, k2tog, k8, k2tog, k1) on each ndl.
Rnd 31: Knit 48.
Rnd 32: (K1, k2tog, k6, k2tog, k1) on each ndl.
Rnd 33: Knit 40.

Rnd 34: (K1, k2tog, k4, k2tog, k1) on each ndl.
Rnd 35: Knit 32.
Rnd 36: (K1, k2tog, k2, k2tog, k1) on each ndl.
Rnd 37: Knit 24.
Rnd 38: (K1, k2tog, k2tog, k1) on each ndl.
Rnd 39: Knit 16.
Rnd 40: (K1, k2tog, k1) on each ndl.
Rnd 41 (the top round with 3 blocks on the chart): Do not knit.
Cut yarn, leaving a tail about 8 in / 20 cm long. Pull through the last 12 sts.
Finishing the ball: Use the tip of your index finger to push the 12 stitches at the top smoothly together as you run your fingertip under the top of the ball. Thread the yarn once more through all the stitches at the top. Bring the needle and yarn through the hole at the top, secure the yarn by pressing the top towards the hole at the base of the ball and sewing it down securely. Steam the ball and fill with wool batting. Thread the yarn through the stitches at the base, tighten, and tie off yarn. When you fill the ball with wool batting, loosen the wool first so the filling is lofty, and then spread it out well inside the ball. Use the index finger to press in fine layers of wool batting. Don't wad the batting when you are stuffing it in the ball because it will clump up.

HANGING LOOPS

Chain 40, leaving a tail long enough to pass through the whole ball. Finish the chain by joining to the first st with a slip stitch. Pull both tails through the last stitch on the hook and sew the tails through the ball.

EASTER EGGS

The eggs are knitted with Heilo yarn as they offer a wide range of colors. We love the holidays it allows us to dress up our dining room where the eggs and balls will hang together on our tree.

Cast on 12 sts over dpn U.S. 2.5 / 3 mm. Divide these 12 sts over 4 dpn = 3 sts per ndl. These stitches are the bottom row of the chart.
Rnd 1: Knit 12.
Rnd 2: (K2, inc 1, k1) on each ndl. [Note: see page 65 for how to increase]
Rnd 3: Knit 16.
Rnd 4: (K1, inc 1, k2, inc 1, k1) on each ndl.
Rnd 5: Knit 24.
Rnd 6: (K1, inc 1, k4, inc 1, k1) on each ndl.
Rnd 7: Knit 32.
Rnd 8: (K1, inc 1, k6, inc 1, k1) on each ndl.
Rnd 9: Knit 40.
Rnd 10: (K1, inc 1, k8, inc 1, k1) on each ndl.
Rnds 11-19: Knit 48.
Rnd 20: (K1, k2tog, k6, k2tog, k1) on each ndl.
Rnds 21-23: Knit 40.
Rnd 24: (K1, k2tog, k4, k2tog, k1) on each ndl.
Rnds 25-27: Knit 32.
Rnd 28: (K1, k2tog, k2, k2tog, k1) on each ndl.
Rnds 29-31: Knit 24.
Rnd 32: (K1, k2tog, k2tog, k1) on each ndl.
Rnds 33-35: Knit 16.
Rnd 36: (K2tog, k2tog) on each ndl. Cut yarn and pull end through remaining 8 sts.

Sew the hole at the bottom of the egg together and then steam the egg before filling it with wool stuffed in from the top. If you are knitting an egg with several colors, weave in the ends as you work so the egg will be smoother.
Run the yarn tail through the stitches at the top of the egg once more and then crochet a hanging loop with 40 chain stitches.
Thread the ends from the hanging loop through the egg from the top down to the base and then secure the ends at the bottom of the egg.

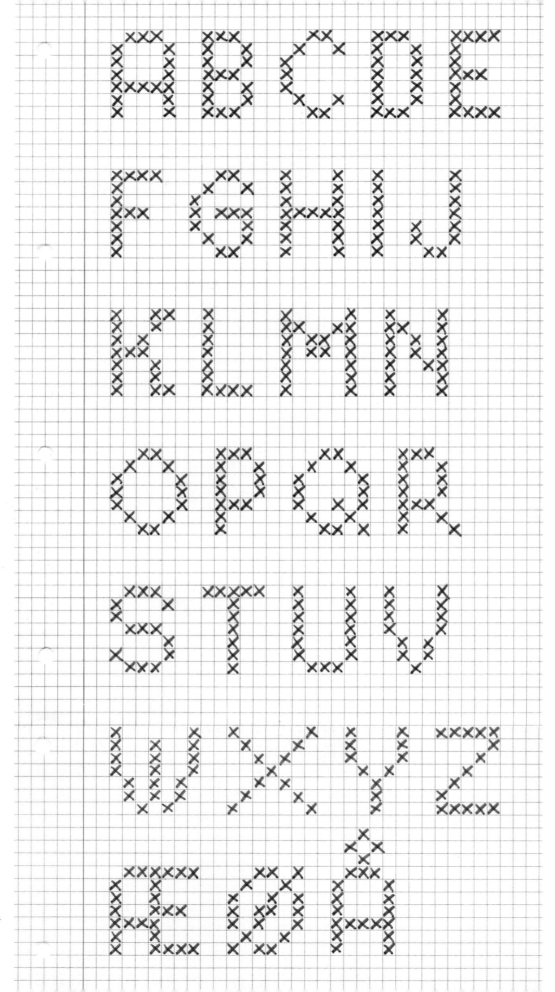

Explanations

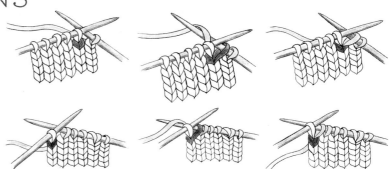

Increasing Stitches

Increase at the beginning of a row by picking up a stitch on the right side of the 2nd stitch on the needle.

Increase at the end of a row by picking up a stitch in the right side of the last stitch on the needle.

Back Stitch

1. When you work the first stitch, decide how long you want to make each stitch.

2. Make the second stitch by inserting the needle half a stitch length from the end of the first stitch and then bring the needle up at the center of the first stitch. Continue the same way to the end of the pattern.

3. When you make the back stitches this way, all the stitches will be the same length. It is very important that the embroidery be worked very smoothly and that the stitches align.

Duplicate Stitch

Sometimes it is easier to embroider a pattern or motif than to knit it in. If you are using only a little bit of a color in a pattern or motif it would be easier to embroider it. If the entire motif needs to be embroidered, mark off a stitch in the knitting that corresponds to a stitch in the motif.

ABBREVIATIONS

BO	bind off (bind off knitwise unless otherwise instructed) (= British cast off)	ndl(s)	needle(s)
		oz	ounce(s)
		p	purl
		psso	pass slipped stitch over
ch	chain (crochet)	rep	repeat
		rnd(s)	round(s)
cm	centimeter(s)	RS	right side
CO	cast on	sc	single crochet (= British double crochet)
dpn	double-pointed needle(s)		
g	gram(s)	sl	slip
k	knit	st(s)	stitch(es)
k2tog	knit 2 together	tbl	through back loop(s)
in	inch(es)		
inc	increase with lifted stitches from row below (see above)	tr	treble crochet (British = double treble)
mm	millimeter(s)	WS	wrong side

  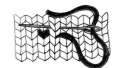